2 X 7/07 LT 6/05
6 X 6/15 LT 6/15

WN

CHINESE
IN AMERICA

web enhanced at www.inamericabooks.com

ALISON BEHNKE

LERNER PUBLICATIONS COMPANY / MINNEAPOLIS

Current information and statistics quickly become out of date. That's why we developed **www.inamericabooks.com**, a companion website to the **In America** series. The site offers lots of additional information—downloadable photos and maps and up-to-date facts through links to additional websites. Each link has been carefully selected by researchers at Lerner Publishing Group and is regularly reviewed and updated. However, Lerner Publishing Group is not responsible for the accuracy or suitability of material on websites that are not maintained directly by us. It is recommended that students using the Internet be supervised by a parent, a librarian, a teacher, or another adult.

Lerner Publications Company
A division of Lerner Publishing Group
241 First Avenue North
Minneapolis, MN 55401 U.S.A.

Website address: www.lernerbooks.com

Library of Congress Cataloging-in-Publication Data

Behnke, Alison.
    Chinese in America / by Alison Behnke.
       p.   cm. — (In America)
    Summary: Examines the history of Chinese immigration to the United States, discussing why they came, what they did when they got here, where they settled, and customs they brought with them.
    Includes bibliographical references and index.
    ISBN: 0–8225–4695–7 (lib. bdg. : alk. paper)
    1. Chinese Americans—History—Juvenile literature. 2. Chinese Americans—Juvenile literature. 3. Immigrants—United States—Juvenile literature. [1. Chinese Americans.] I. Title. II. In America (Minneapolis, Minn.)
    E184.C5 B45 2005
    973.04'951—dc21   2002010676

Manufactured in the United States of America
1 2 3 4 5 6 – JR – 10 09 08 07 06 05

CONTENTS

INTRODUCTION

In America, a walk down a city street can seem like a walk through many lands. Grocery stores sell international foods. Shops offer products from around the world. People strolling past may speak foreign languages. This unique blend of cultures is the result of America's history as a nation of immigrants.

Native peoples have lived in North America for centuries. The next settlers were the Vikings. In about A.D. 1000, they sailed from Scandinavia to lands that would become Canada, Greenland, and Iceland. In 1492 the Italian navigator Christopher Columbus landed in the Americas, and more European explorers arrived during the 1500s. In the 1600s, British settlers formed colonies that, after the Revolutionary War (1775–1783), would become the United States. And in the mid-1800s, a great wave of immigration brought millions of new arrivals to the young country.

Immigrants have many different reasons for leaving home. They may leave to escape poverty, war, or harsh governments. They may want better living conditions for themselves and their children. Throughout its history, America has been known as a nation that offers many opportunities. For this reason, many immigrants come to America.

Moving to a new country is not easy. It can mean making a long, difficult journey. It means leaving home and starting over in an unfamiliar place. But it also means using skill, talent, and determination to build a new life. The In America series tells the story of immigration to the United States and the search for fresh beginnings in a new country—in America.

CHINESE IN AMERICA

According to the 2000 U.S. census, nearly 2.4 million Chinese Americans live in the United States. That population has its origins in the 1840s and 1850s, when large numbers of Chinese immigrants first began to arrive in America. Attracted by stories of gold in California, many Chinese left poverty and hardship in their homeland. They hoped to earn enough money in America to provide better lives for their families.

At first, Chinese immigrants struggled with prejudice, discrimination, and violence in their new country. But, despite the obstacles, Chinese Americans went on to make important contributions to science, art, literature, music, film, and business in their new country. In the 1990s and 2000s, new waves of Chinese immigrants arrived in America. Like earlier immigrants, they were unhappy with China's government and economy. With dreams of the future, these future Chinese Americans left home to look for opportunities in America.

1

FROM THE LAND OF THE DRAGON

China is a huge nation. It stretches all the way across the eastern half of Asia to the China Sea. Southeastern China is warm and humid, while the northern part of the country has long, snowy winters. Mountains, deserts, seashores, and valleys all make up this diverse country. Amazing animals, from camels to giant pandas, live in China's wilderness. The nation's capital is Beijing, a large city in northeastern China.

AN ANCIENT LAND

China has thousands of years of recorded history behind it. In fact, scientists think that some of the earliest humans on earth lived in China more than one million years ago. In about the 1700s B.C., people in China began keeping records of their government and their lives. From those writings, modern historians know that Chinese history is divided into dynasties. During each dynasty, one royal family held power. Sometimes many generations of the same family ruled during a dynasty.

The Shang dynasty, during which the Shang family ruled, began in about 1770 B.C. Stories are told about earlier dynasties, but no one knows exactly where the legends end and the facts begin. During the early Shang dynasty, people in China used a system of writing, rode in horse-drawn chariots, and made beautiful works of art out of bronze and jade.

After the Shang dynasty ended in the 1100s or 1000s, the Zhou family took power. The Zhou dynasty lasted until 256 B.C. Confucius, a famous philosopher, lived during this period. Confucius and his followers believed that good government and a good society depended on order and duty. After Confucius's death, his students wrote

This two-headed bronze vessel from the Shang dynasty may have been a teapot.

Confucius had many students who wrote down his teachings on proper behavior.

books about proper, or ethical, behavior for leaders. These books, which are called the Confucian classics, helped shape Chinese culture and society. People around the world still study these important works.

China was made up of many small kingdoms until 221 B.C. In that year, Qin Shi Huangdi joined all the kingdoms together. Many other dynasties followed the Qin dynasty, and Chinese society made great advances. The Han dynasty (ca. 202 B.C. to A.D. 220) and the Tang dynasty (A.D. 600s to 800s) were especially productive periods. Leaders developed complex systems of government. Doctors used new medicines and treatments to heal their patients.

WONDERFUL WORKS

While Qin Shi Huangdi was emperor, he ordered workers to begin building what became one of China's most famous features—the Great Wall. Laborers joined together older, smaller walls built during earlier dynasties. They also added new sections, building them from stone and dirt. The wall eventually stretched for thousands of miles across northern China, protecting the country's border from invaders.

Qin Shi Huangdi also left behind another treasure. Archaeologists who explored his large tomb found an army of more than eight thousand life-size figures. Made from a special kind of clay called terra-cotta, the soldiers all have detailed uniforms. Some of them even have terra-cotta horses. Each statue is different, and historians think that royal artists made them to look like Qin Shi Huangdi's own troops.

The Great Wall winds and twists over many hills and mountains in China.

Artists and writers created beautiful works. Scientists and engineers invented movable type, paper, fireworks, and the magnetic compass.

NEW INFLUENCES

Surrounded by steep mountains, broad deserts, and great oceans, China was difficult for many travelers to reach. But over time, China did make connections with other lands and other people. Chinese sailors and explorers made long journeys to distant regions. Merchants created a trade route over land to countries in western Asia and in Europe. They carried Chinese silk and other goods along this route, called the Silk Road, to parts of an ancient civilization called the Roman Empire. Other Chinese traders journeyed to southern Asia to sell their wares. Traders came to China too, bringing new ideas and new cultures.

Genghis Khan (below) was a clever military commander. His tactics in battle remain in use in modern times.

Not all visitors to China were welcome. In the 1200s, a warrior and leader named Genghis Khan swept in from Mongolia, a region to the north. Genghis Khan and

MING MAJESTY

Mongol rule in China lasted from the 1200s to the mid-1300s. Then a new Chinese dynasty, called the Ming dynasty, took power in China. During Ming rule, China developed further. Workers built many temples and palaces in Beijing. Sailors made long journeys. Rulers and businesspeople welcomed leaders and traders from faraway lands. Authors wrote great novels. Builders restored and expanded the Great Wall.

The Ming dynasty is also very famous for its art. Artists discovered new ways to make pottery during the Ming period. They created beautiful blue and white vases *(right)* that became very highly prized.

his descendants, including Kublai Khan, invaded and conquered China. The country remained part of the Mongol Empire for nearly two hundred years.

In the 1400s, another new influence arrived in China. European sailors and adventurers were roaming the world in search of riches and new lands. European merchants and rulers hired sea captains to find a sea route to eastern Asia. One of these sailors was Christopher Columbus. Blown off course, he landed in the New World of the Americas in 1492. He never made it to Asia. But soon after Columbus's voyage, European merchants successfully landed in Guangzhou (Canton), the only

While China's borders have shifted over the years, this map shows the country as it appears in modern times. Download this and other maps at www.inamericabooks.com.

Chinese port that foreigners were allowed to enter. The Portuguese reached Guangzhou in 1516, the Dutch arrived in 1624, and the British came in 1637.

Chinese merchants were happy to trade China's silks, porcelain, tea, and works of art for the furs, sandalwood, food, and herbs that European merchants offered. This trade took place in Macao and Guangzhou, cities on China's southern coast.

However, the Chinese were protective of their culture and their country. They did not want Europeans to try to change anything in China. When the Chinese allowed European traders into the country, the traders stayed in a separate area outside the city walls of Guangzhou. They were rarely allowed to leave the trading compound. When they did leave, they had to be with Chinese guides.

One or two adventurous traders did sneak into Guangzhou in disguise. They brought back colorful tales of a lively city. Beautiful and frightening new sights and sounds were everywhere in Guangzhou. The foreigners saw enormous statues and heard the deep sound of gongs. They smelled burning incense. They saw flower-decked boats for rulers and their attendants, and they witnessed battles between street gangs. They passed fish sellers walking through the streets, carrying their fish in tubs of water hanging from bamboo poles.

The United States became an independent nation in 1783. The next year, American shippers eagerly began doing business in China. Trade between China and the United States grew quickly. American merchants from Massachusetts, Rhode Island, New York, Pennsylvania, and

Maryland sailed to Guangzhou. They sold birds' nests and sharks' fins for soups, tortoiseshell and mother-of-pearl for ornaments, and sandalwood for perfume. They offered Chinese buyers furs from Alaska and Canada.

The Americans were glad to buy Chinese items too. They bought teakwood chests, lacquered tables, jade and ivory ornaments, porcelain, silks, and bronze. They also brought back chinoiserie—Chinese-style art and decorations. These goods were very popular at home in the United States.

An American flag (**second from right**) *flies in this busy Chinese seaport.*

TROUBLED TIMES

During this period, many other nations were also trading with China. British traders began shipping opium from India and selling it in China. Chinese doctors originally used opium as a medicine to ease pain. However, it is also a highly addictive drug, and soon the British opium trade was booming. By 1800 many of China's 250 million people had become addicted to opium. They were spending large amounts of money on the drug. To fight the problem, China's emperor passed a law forbidding opium to be imported into the country. British traders formally agreed to follow the emperor's law. But they continued to provide the drug through a large illegal trade.

During the Opium War, Chinese ships (left and right) are ready to fight the approaching European ship (center).

Finally, the Chinese government decided to wipe out the opium trade for good. A Chinese official traveled to Guangzhou and ordered all foreign and Chinese traders to stop dealing in opium. Anyone who disobeyed the rule would be sentenced to death. This punishment would affect anyone who grew, sold, or smoked opium. British, American, and other traders didn't want to obey. The British, who still had large amounts of opium to sell, were very upset about the ban.

Chinese officials seized and destroyed the valuable supplies of opium. Angry British traders fought back. Britain sent ships and soldiers to China in 1839, and the Opium War began. The British forces overpowered the Chinese army, and the Chinese emperor surrendered. After the war, China and Britain signed the Nanking Treaty. This treaty required China to give land to the British, to open up new ports to international trade, and to pay a large fine. On top of it all, the opium trade began again.

After the Opium War, China was more reluctant than ever to let outsiders into the country. But the conflict had opened the nation to greater foreign influence. Many more Europeans began arriving, traveling from countries such as England, France, Germany, and Russia. American merchants, missionaries (religious teachers),

> *There are those [in Britain] who smuggle opium to seduce the Chinese people and so cause the spread of the poison to the provinces. His Majesty the Emperor, upon hearing of this, is in a towering rage. He has especially sent me . . . to investigate and settle this matter.*
>
> *—from a letter to Britain's Queen Victoria from the Chinese emperor's commissioner Lin Tue-Hsü, 1839*

political figures, and teachers also came. The foreigners lived in separate communities called Little Americas. These settlements were soon scattered throughout China. They were protected by outside treaties, and they had their own rules. They did not always follow China's laws. Many Chinese were unhappy with the presence of the Little Americas.

China also had other problems during the mid–1800s. The Manchu dynasty had ruled the country since 1644. Many of the government's leaders were dishonest and cruel.

Most Chinese farmers and workers were very poor. But the wealthy Manchu rulers made them pay high taxes, forcing the population further into poverty.

Conditions grew worse in China in the 1850s. A secret society called the Taipings had managed to gather support from many of the common people. When they attacked the Manchus in Beijing, civil war broke out. The battles of the Taiping Rebellion raged for years, killing more than twenty million people. Hundreds of Chinese cities and

Millions of people died during the fourteen-year-long Taiping Rebellion.

Wealthy Chinese families in the mid-1800s had time to enjoy popular hobbies such as flying kites (above).

villages were destroyed. Soldiers robbed people of the little money or food that they had set aside. The countryside was devastated.

DAILY LIFE

By the 1850s, more than 400 million people lived in China. Some of these people were wealthy. Most rich families lived in the cities. They had large, luxurious homes with iron gates, inner courtyards, and clear pools filled with goldfish. Some wealthy people came

from noble families. Others had made fortunes in business or trade.

But many more Chinese were very poor. Most of them lived in small villages in the country. They built their homes themselves, forming walls out of earth and stone and covering them with straw roofs. They planted crops such as rice, wheat, and beans, using simple equipment pulled by cows, water buffalo, or oxen. Some farmers raised pigs, chickens, or ducks.

Farming was hard, and harvests were often very small. Many Chinese struggled to feed their families. Meals in country homes were usually simple. People ate rice and noodles at every meal, and soup was a common dish. If they could afford

Yoked to a wheel and turning it by pacing around and around, an ox powers a simple irrigation system on a farm near Shanghai.

FIND LINKS TO LEARN MORE ABOUT DAILY LIFE IN CHINA AT WWW.INAMERICABOOKS.COM.

it, most Chinese enjoyed tea. For holidays and celebrations, families might splurge on special foods such as meat dishes and sweets.

Chinese households were often large, and families were very close-knit. Three or even four generations usually lived together under one roof. Couples had many children to help work in the fields and around the house.

Severe famines (periods without enough food), droughts (dry spells), and floods made life even harder for people in China. And conflicts such as the Opium War and the Taiping Rebellion made China's poor farmers and workers even poorer. Facing poverty and war, many Chinese looked for ways to improve their lives. When they heard of opportunities for work and good pay overseas, they listened.

LEAVING HOME

In the 1840s and 1850s, it was against the law for Chinese citizens to emigrate, or to move to another country. But many nations were looking for workers. So Chinese laborers traveled illegally to Asian countries such as Siam (present-day Thailand), Burma (also called Myanmar), Vietnam, and the Philippines.

Other Chinese made a much longer journey. They went to the United States. In America California was beginning to attract many settlers. Gold had been discovered there in 1848. As word spread of gold in the California hills, fortune hunters from all over the world—including China—headed to San Francisco as fast as they could.

People said going to America was like going to Heaven.

—Law Ying, from Chinese American Portraits: Personal Histories 1828–1988

Chinese merchants in San Francisco soon carried home news of the gold strike in California. In Chinese villages, stories spread about the Gum San—the "Gold Mountain"—where gold was lying on the ground just waiting to be picked up. Many Chinese disobeyed the government's rule against leaving the country. They set sail for San Francisco.

Most of these Chinese emigrants hoped to find gold. Others planned to work on farms or to find jobs in the many new industries on the West Coast of the United States. At that time, unskilled laborers in California could make one to five dollars a day. This was a lot of money for Chinese workers, who had been lucky to get ten cents a day back home.

Chinese emigrants did not always have a clear idea of what lay ahead. Some of them did not even want to leave China. For example, some countries sent people to kidnap Chinese workers and force them to work abroad. In other cases, agents from

False promises tricked many Chinese laborers to agree to leave China. Thousands of them lived in camps, such as this one near the port city of Macao in 1857, while waiting for the ships that would take them abroad.

Passengers and cargo headed for the United States wait to board a ship.

international companies persuaded workers to leave China by making false promises about the life ahead. The agents knew that many workers had a hard time finding good jobs in America. But they told Chinese workers that they would earn a lot of money and live in nice houses.

Other Chinese didn't want to leave their homes and loved ones. But many poor men felt it was their duty to leave home to earn money to support their families in China. They left reluctantly, but almost all of them felt sure that they would return home again. Approximately 300,000 Chinese immigrants entered the United

> *Fong Dun Shung hoisted his Gold Mountain bag onto his shoulder and nodded one last time to his wife, daughter, and . . . sons. . . . How long, he wondered, would it be before [he] returned home?*
>
> —Lisa See, a Chinese American author, **On Gold Mountain**, *1995*

States between 1840 and 1882. More than half of them returned to China within a few years.

MAKING THE JOURNEY

Arranging trips from China to California soon became highly organized and very profitable. Most people traveled from Hong Kong, a region to the south of China. In Hong Kong, they borrowed money from Chinese agents called brokers, who offered loans to pay for the trip. The voyage itself cost about fifty dollars. But the brokers charged extra fees. Sometimes these fees raised the price to as much as two hundred dollars—a huge sum for a Chinese farmer. Many Chinese agreed to pay. They were sure they would soon be rich enough to repay the loan. However, their dreams did not always come true, and it often took five or six years for people to pay for their trips.

Some Chinese emigrants were lucky enough to make the voyage comfortably in fast ships. Many others had a long, miserable journey in old, rundown ships. The trip from Hong Kong to California could take four months or longer. Many travelers got seasick. Other sicknesses were quickly passed from passenger to passenger in the overcrowded quarters. Passengers had little room to eat or to sleep.

In these cramped, uncomfortable conditions, many Chinese emigrants tried to make the best of things. They passed the time with new friends whom they met on the trip. They shared memories. They told stories of their homes and families in China. And they talked about the future, imagining America and what life would be like in the new land that lay at the end of their journey.

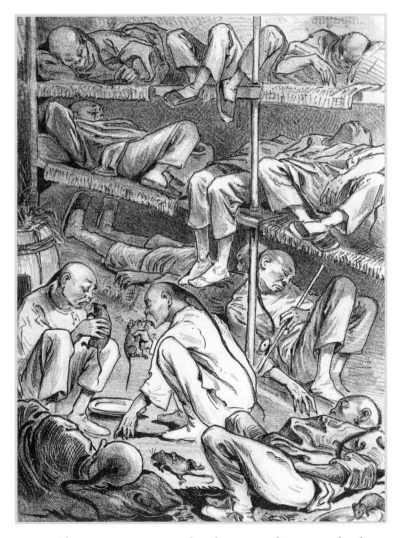

Many Chinese immigrants endured grim conditions on the ships that carried them to the United States.

2 To the Land of the Gold Mountain

When Chinese immigrants landed in San Francisco, they were often tired or sick from the long voyage. The new land where they found themselves was unfamiliar. It was an overwhelming experience.

But Chinese soon found that they were not completely alone in the Land of the Gold Mountain. Representatives of the Chinese Six Companies welcomed them to their new home. The Chinese Six represented the six districts in Guangdong, the province from which most Chinese immigrants came. They sorted new arrivals into groups of people who spoke the same dialect, or regional variation of the Chinese language. They also offered them places to stay in local dormitories. Immigrants usually lived with people who were from the same area back home. These newcomers were happy to have some familiar company. San Francisco did not always seem like a very friendly or safe place. The streets were full of gambling and fighting. Living in San Francisco was expensive, as well. Immigrants helped each other face the challenges of their new lives.

A HOME AWAY FROM HOME

Most of the Chinese immigrants pouring into San Francisco were male. They had come to the United States alone, planning to return to China with their fortunes or to bring their families to America later. They found housing in shared bunkhouses and dormitories and looked for work. Some eventually earned enough money and decided to bring their wives and children over from China. Still, there weren't very many Chinese women in the United States. For the few women who did live in the community, life was quiet. Most women spent their time caring for children and doing housework.

Chinese immigrants pose on the steps of a tenement (run-down apartment building) in San Francisco's Chinatown in 1888.

As more and more Chinese people settled in San Francisco, a whole neighborhood, known as Chinatown, developed. Chinese businesses began to appear on the city's streets. Chinese grocery stores sold familiar foods from home.

Restaurants opened and became popular meeting places where people sat at tables and ate or played Chinese games such as fan-tan and mah-jongg. Shrines and temples offered people places to worship.

CUSTOMS AND COMMUNITY

Religion has traditionally been an important part of Chinese life. The most widespread religions in China are Buddhism and Taoism. People may blend these two faiths or combine them with ancient religious

These Chinese immigrants are dressed up to celebrate a traditional Chinese New Year in 1911.

customs that are older than either Buddhism or Taoism. Confucian philosophy has also been a major influence on Chinese society.

Many Chinese holidays are based on Buddhism and have been celebrated for hundreds of years. Chinese people of all beliefs often share in the festivities. Traditional celebrations usually involve family meals and activities. Community events such as music, dance, or services at shrines or temples are also popular.

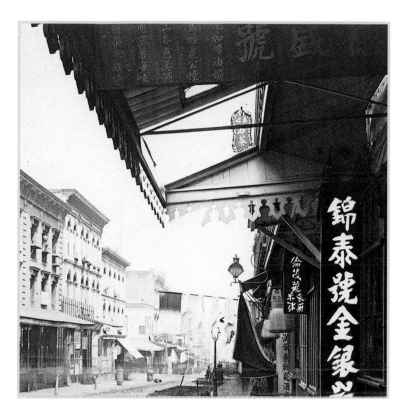

Chinese-language signs in San Francisco's Chinatown looked familiar to new arrivals.

Many people gathered in *fongs*—places where people from the same region in China met to chat and to play cards. People who were out of work or visiting from other towns could eat and sleep at the fongs. Immigrants could get their mail at their fongs, and they could choose to pay into and borrow money from the fongs' shared banks.

Family associations also formed in the Chinese immigrant community. These groups were made up of people with the same family name. Fewer than five hundred different family names existed in China. People felt a bond with others who shared their name. Like the fongs, these family associations provided housing and food. The associations often paid funeral expenses for members who died without any close family in the United States. The associations also provided interpreters, settled arguments, and held celebrations for important festivals. Members of the associations helped to pay for these services.

To find links to learn more about life in American Chinatowns, visit www.inamericabooks.com.

Fongs and family associations sent representatives to bigger groups called Chinese benevolent associations. The Chinese Six Companies eventually became a benevolent association in San Francisco. They set up rules and guidelines for the Chinese community. They also helped the Chinese neighborhood deal with the city government. The group worked hard to make life better for Chinese people in America.

San Francisco had the first Chinatown in the United States. But a few Chinese gradually began to settle in other places around the country, where they formed new Chinatowns.

This tiny Chinatown was located in Deadwood, South Dakota.

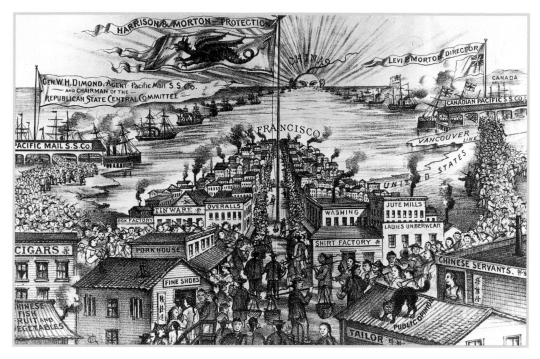

In this anti-Chinese cartoon, immigrants pour into San Francisco's Chinatown. The black cat labeled "public opinion" (**lower right**) *represents the hostilities that the Chinese immigrants faced. Many Californians saw them as threats to American jobs and culture.*

Glad to have a warm, familiar community, many immigrants rarely left Chinatown. Some Americans did not like the way that most Chinese lived apart from other people. They thought that the Chinese did not want to try to fit into American society. But the Chinese had many reasons for keeping to themselves. Outside of Chinatowns, they often faced prejudice. Chinese immigrants dressed, spoke, and ate differently than most Americans.

Sometimes these differences led to discrimination and hostility. Strong families were important to the Chinese. Yet most laborers had left their families behind. They were alone in a new country, facing a new way of life. But living together in Chinatowns, the Chinese were able to keep their traditional culture and customs alive in their new country.

LIMITED BY THE LAW

Between the 1850s and 1870s, California passed many laws that discriminated against Chinese immigrants. Eventually, these laws were repealed (overturned). But while they lasted, they made life very difficult for the Chinese in America.

- **The Foreign Miners' Tax** was passed in 1852, during California's gold rush. The law charged foreign miners in California twenty dollars a month. All immigrants who had mining jobs were supposed to pay the tax. Most miners moved around a lot and did not have permanent addresses. It was hard to identify and track down these workers and make them pay the fee. But since officials could tell that Chinese were foreigners by their appearance, most Chinese miners had to pay.

Miners who had emigrated from Europe (left) *found it easier to avoid the Foreign Miners' Tax than did Chinese miners* (right).

- **The Cubic Air Ordinance** of 1871 said that each adult in San Francisco had to have at least five hundred cubic feet of living space. Housing was cramped in Chinatown, and the police arrested hundreds of Chinese people for breaking the ordinance (law). Before long, the jails became so overcrowded that they also violated the law. The city soon had to repeal the Cubic Air Ordinance.

- **The Queue Ordinance** was introduced in 1873. In China at that time, Chinese men were required to wear their hair in long pigtails called queues. In order to be sure that they could return to China if they wanted to, Chinese men kept their queues. But the new law forced all prisoners in San Francisco jails—some of whom were Chinese—to cut their hair to one inch in length.

- **The Laundry Ordinance** of the 1870s charged laundry businesses in San Francisco a fee every three months. Laundries with one-horse vehicles paid two dollars. Laundries with two-horse vehicles paid four dollars. And laundries with no horse-drawn vehicles paid fifteen dollars. Many Chinese people in San Francisco were involved in the laundry business. Since they carried clothes in baskets rather than using horse-drawn carts, they had to pay the highest fee.

To learn more about Chinese miners and the California goldfields, visit WWW.INAMERICABOOKS.COM for links.

In the Goldfields

After finding homes, the next important thing for new immigrants was finding work. In the 1840s and 1850s, most of them had come to the United States to work in California's goldfields. But the immigrants' dreams of fortune and success in the Land of the Gold Mountain did not always come true. Life in the goldfields was rough, tough, and very competitive. The people who got there first staked claims (chose plots of land) and went over the ground in search of large pieces of gold. Then they moved on to fresh claims.

When Chinese immigrants arrived in San Francisco on their way to the goldfields, the Chinese Six Companies gave them advice about their choices. They could stake claims in the goldfields and work on their own. They could also work as assistants to miners who already had claims. Assistants got to keep half of all the gold that they found. Or, if they preferred, Chinese immigrants could take jobs in the mining camps. They could also work in San Francisco as skilled carpenters or in laundries, restaurants, or hotels. These jobs did not sound as exciting as looking for gold, but sometimes they paid good, steady wages.

Many Chinese who became miners made rich strikes and good incomes. Others worked patiently and carefully to find enough gold dust and small pieces of gold to make them rich. But the work wasn't easy, and fellow workers could be

You could see the Chinese everywhere, but you never heard about the role they played in building the West.

—*Philip Choy, from* Chinese American Portraits, *1988*

These Chinese railroad workers in California are wearing traditional Chinese hats and shirts.

unfriendly. People sometimes fought over the best claims. And other miners often made cruel jokes about the Chinese. The Chinese were set apart by their physical appearance and by their traditional Chinese clothes—blue blouses, baggy trousers, cloth slippers, and wide straw hats. Chinese men also wore waist-long pigtails known as queues. It hurt the Chinese workers' feelings and pride when others made fun of them. But they kept working.

In the early years of the gold rush, many Chinese immigrants returned home after a while. They took the money they had made back to their villages. But some of them found it hard to settle down again in China. They returned to the California goldfields. As time passed, however, it got harder to stake good claims. Much of the ground had been worked over. Miners began to return home or to take other jobs. Eventually, the goldfields of California were nearly used up.

BUILDING THE RAILROAD

When the gold began to run out, Chinese immigrants had to look for new work. They found it in a great construction project. In 1862 President Abraham

Lincoln approved the building of a new railroad. It would link the East Coast of the United States to the West Coast. The Union Pacific Company would lay the tracks heading westward out of Omaha, Nebraska. The Central Pacific Company would start building eastward from California.

The work was slow and difficult. Laying railroad ties meant cutting down trees, digging out stumps, breaking apart rock and carting it to different sites, laying down the wooden railroad ties, and pounding in the metal rails. Heavy machinery had not been invented yet, so all of the labor had to be done by hand. Workers used picks, shovels, crowbars, axes, sledgehammers, blasting powder, wheelbarrows, and horse-drawn carts.

The railroad companies needed thousands of laborers to do this enormous job. But at first the companies had trouble luring men away from the riches of the California goldfields. Once the companies had found construction crews, few workers stayed on the job for more than one week. Charles Crocker, the director of construction for the Central Pacific Company, had an idea. In 1865 he asked the Chinese Six Companies to help him find five thousand workers.

The Chinese Six Companies helped the Central Pacific find and hire workers in San Francisco's Chinatown and other places along the West Coast. The Chinese soon earned a reputation as dedicated and energetic workers. They helped to produce the

WE WORKED EVERY DAY UNTIL LATE. . . . WE DIDN'T EVEN NOTICE WHEN THE SUN ROSE OR WHEN THE DAY FELL.

—*Jone Ho Leong, from* Bitter Melon, *1987*

CHECK OUT WWW.INAMERICABOOKS.COM FOR LINKS TO MORE INFORMATION ON THE EXPERIENCES OF CHINESE LABORERS IN AMERICA.

longest and smoothest stretches of track through the rugged mountains of the Sierra Nevada.

As the construction crews moved higher into the Sierra Nevada, the mountains grew steeper. It became harder and harder to cut a path through the stony slopes. Chinese workers found a way to solve this problem. Using reeds from San Francisco Bay, they wove round baskets with waist–high sides. One or two Chinese workmen were lowered in these baskets by rope and pulley down the side of a sheer cliff. The workers chipped holes in the rock and packed in blasting powder. Then they were quickly hauled to safety before the powder exploded. The blasts created gaps that the workers could use to carve out the railroad's bed. But this work was very dangerous, and many Chinese laborers lost their lives.

By 1866 ten thousand Chinese were working on the railroad. The Chinese laborers organized themselves into crews of twelve to twenty men, often keeping a few spare workers in case someone got sick. Life in the workers' camps was simple. Each crew lived together in tents or huts. Each crew had its own cook and its own leader, who kept order among the workmen. Chinese workers brought their own groceries to camp. They ate foods such as dried oysters, bamboo shoots, bean sprouts, crackers, noodles, Chinese bacon and pork, poultry, and tea.

Each night, high in the mountains . . . Chinese [railroad] laborers gathered around the campfire. One night there might be a game of dow ngow. . . . Occasionally they were entertained by fiddlers or flutists. . . . On some nights, professional storytellers regaled them with tales.

—Lisa See, On Gold Mountain, *1995*

In 1869 the eastern and western sections of the railroad met in Utah. The railroad was finished. The workers' camps emptied out. Almost overnight, twenty-five thousand men lost their jobs and began competing with each other for whatever other work was available. Many Chinese workers returned to China. Others went to Hawaii to work on large sugarcane farms called plantations.

At the same time, even more Chinese immigrants were arriving in the United States. Many took jobs picking fruit, tomatoes, and other produce. However, most of this farmwork was seasonal, leaving thousands of Chinese unemployed for months at a time. Some immigrants took jobs in factories. Others became servants in private homes or worked in city restaurants, hotels, or shops.

FONG DUN SHUNG OFTEN THOUGHT OF THOSE LAST FEW DAYS ON THE RAILROAD— HOW THE MEN HAD BEEN FILLED WITH EXCITEMENT AS THEY RUSHED TO BE THE FIRST TEAM TO FINISH, HOW ONCE IT WAS OVER NO ONE KNEW QUITE WHAT TO DO.

—*Lisa See,* On Gold Mountain, *1995*

A restaurant in New York City employed these Chinese immigrants in the early twentieth century.

36

FORTUNE COOKIES

Many people think that fortune cookies come from China, but in fact they were probably invented in San Francisco's Chinatown. Make these treats for a taste of Chinese American culture. To make the fortunes, cut white paper into 25 strips about 2 inches long and ³⁄₄-inch wide and write a saying or prediction on each one. For a taste of other traditional Chinese and Chinese American recipes, check out www.inamericabooks.com.

1 C. MARGARINE, SOFTENED	2¹⁄₂ TSP. VANILLA EXTRACT
¹⁄₂ C. SUGAR	3¹⁄₄ C. FLOUR
1 EGG	¹⁄₂ TSP. BAKING POWDER

1. Preheat the oven to 425°F. In a large bowl, combine margarine, sugar, egg, and vanilla. Mix until smooth. Add flour and baking powder. Stir well until you have a firm dough.
2. Lightly flour a clean countertop or other work surface. Use a rolling pin to roll dough to about ¹⁄₈-inch thick. Use a circle-shaped cookie cutter or the top of a drinking glass (about 2¹⁄₂ inches wide) to cut out circles in dough.
3. Put a fortune in each circle, off to one side. Fold the circle in half and then in half again. Pinch it to close. Repeat with remaining dough and fortunes.
4. Place cookies on an ungreased baking sheet and bake for 10 minutes, or until lightly browned.

Makes about 25 cookies

FIGHTING FOR A PLACE

People kept streaming into California looking for jobs. But thousands of people were out of work. The few available jobs were hard to get, and pay was low. The Chinese, along with other workers, were hit hard by the tough economic situation.

Even when Chinese immigrants found jobs, they faced challenges. Some people also accused the Chinese of taking jobs away from Americans. Frustrated workers attacked Chinese immigrants. Riots against the Chinese took place in cities around the United States. Mobs set fire to Chinese neighborhoods in San Francisco and other cities.

Chinese immigrants did not have very many legal rights in America. It was hard for them to protect themselves from this kind of violence and discrimination. When they had first arrived, Chinese immigrants had not been allowed to become U.S. citizens or to vote. In some states, they were not protected by the courts. For example, California passed a law saying that "people of color"— Asians, Africans, African

Violent assaults on Chinese immigrants were not limited to California. Residents of Denver, Colorado, attacked local Chinese residents (below) in 1880.

Americans, and Native Americans—could not testify against white people in court.

In 1869 a group of San Francisco citizens formed the Chinese Protective Society to help keep Chinese immigrants safe from violence. They hired special police guards and met Chinese people arriving on ships. But the society received very little public support or money, and it only lasted for one year.

Soon afterwards, in 1871, the Chinese American community in nearby Los Angeles experienced some of the worst anti–Chinese violence yet, called the Chinese Massacre. What began as an argument erupted into a riot. A group of about five hundred Los Angeles residents attacked the Chinese community. Nineteen Chinese American men and boys were killed.

CHINATOWNS ACROSS THE COUNTRY

Tragedies such as the Chinese Massacre led some Chinese people on the West Coast to try to fight for their rights. However, these individuals had little support and even less success. Faced with what seemed like a losing battle, many of them went home to China. Others went to large cities in New England, the Midwest, or the South.

Many Chinese moved from the West Coast to New York City, and a large Chinatown soon appeared there. New York's Chinatown grew quickly. By 1887 it had about one thousand inhabitants. Many of them lived in old, overcrowded buildings.

Life in the streets of America's Chinatowns wasn't always quiet. The community faced crime and other social problems. Many American police did not try to enforce local laws in Chinatowns. Instead, they let the communities take care of their own problems. But some of the Chinese authorities who were supposed to keep law and order committed crimes themselves. Tongs, secret societies that had started in China, also broke the laws. Wars between the tongs frequently broke out in American Chinatowns.

CLOSING THE DOOR

Beginning in the 1880s, new laws made it harder for Chinese people to come to America. For example, the United States passed the Chinese Exclusion Act in 1882. This law prevented most Chinese immigrants from entering the country. Students, teachers, merchants, and government officials from China could still immigrate. But laborers, who were the biggest group of immigrants, could not enter.

Other laws also limited Chinese immigration. In 1888 the Scott Act said that Chinese people who left the United States could not return. This act separated thousands of Chinese laborers from their homes and jobs. The Geary Act of 1892 required all Chinese living in the United States to get certificates of registration. Under this act, Chinese people had to show their registration certificates whenever officials asked them to do so. If they did not have certificates, they could be sent back to China. The Immigration Act of 1924 prevented the Chinese wives of immigrants from coming to the United States.

Some Chinese disobeyed these laws, which together were known as exclusion laws. They wanted to look for work in the United States so much that they came into the country illegally. Smugglers charged high prices to forge papers and to sneak immigrants across the border from Canada, Mexico, or Cuba. Smuggling became more dangerous when Canada and Mexico passed their own exclusion laws.

But even with their problems, Chinatowns usually helped their people. These neighborhoods had Chinese theaters, restaurants, grocery stores, schools, temples, banks, laundries, and shops. Chinese businesspeople hired Chinese employees and served Chinese customers. Communities also celebrated holidays and festivals. These events helped immigrants keep up the traditional customs of their homeland.

Other Chinatowns continued to form all over the United States throughout the late 1800s, in cities from Honolulu, Hawaii, to Boston, Massachusetts. Immigrants continued to go wherever there was work, and Chinatowns appeared wherever there were many Chinese immigrants.

Some of these communities were short-lived. Most of the Chinatowns that had formed in mining and railroad communities disappeared when the work ran out. Construction and development destroyed other Chinatowns. Still others shrank as Chinese Americans moved to the suburbs and joined larger American communities. But many Chinatowns survived. They gave Chinese Americans a place of their own, a home away from home where the way of life was familiar and reassuring.

MANY PEOPLE ARE INTERESTED IN LEARNING ABOUT THEIR FAMILY'S HISTORY. THIS STUDY IS CALLED GENEALOGY. IF YOU'D LIKE TO LEARN ABOUT YOUR OWN GENEALOGY AND HOW YOUR ANCESTORS CAME TO AMERICA, VISIT WWW.INAMERICABOOKS.COM FOR TIPS AND LINKS TO HELP YOU GET STARTED.

3

A CENTURY OF CHANGE

By the beginning of the 1900s, Chinese immigrants had already made a lot of progress in America. They had worked hard and overcome obstacles. But many challenges still lay ahead. As Chinese Americans thought about the new century, they wondered what the future had in store.

NEW GENERATIONS

A new generation of Chinese Americans was growing up in the United States in the early 1900s. Many of them had been born in America. They didn't feel the same need for Chinatown communities as their older relatives had. They became less and less connected to traditional family ways and ancient Chinese culture. They spoke English and they went to American schools. Many of them went on to college after finishing high school. In college they learned about new opportunities. They received training for different kinds of jobs than they could find in Chinatown.

Young Chinese American women became less likely to accept their traditional roles as homemakers and mothers. They wanted the freedom to live and work wherever they wished. More and more Chinese Americans married people of other ethnic backgrounds.

All of these factors led to large numbers of Chinese Americans leaving Chinatowns for good.

THE EARTH DRAGON TREMBLES IN SAN FRANCISCO

On April 18, 1906, a little after five o'clock in the morning, a massive earthquake roared through San Francisco. The earth shook under the city. Buildings trembled and collapsed. Cobblestone streets cracked and opened up. Walls crashed to the ground.

People in Chinatown and the rest of San Francisco rushed from crumbling buildings into the streets. Overturned lamps and broken gas lines started flames that swept the city. By nightfall all of Chinatown was on fire. People streamed out of the area, holding bundles of whatever possessions they could carry. The fires continued to blaze for three days.

When the danger was past, the city had to be rebuilt. San Francisco businesspeople made good offers to buy Chinatown's valuable land. But the Chinese would not sell. Instead, they set to work rebuilding their homes and businesses themselves.

Neighborhood populations shrank rapidly, and some Chinatowns disappeared completely. In addition, fewer Chinese immigrants were coming into the country. For a while, it looked as if Chinatowns might vanish.

Chinatowns faced new challenges when, in 1917, the United States joined an international conflict called World War I (1914–1918). American families of all heritages faced wartime hardships, such as sending loved ones off to fight and getting by with limited supplies.

MY PARENTS WANTED ME TO GROW UP A GOOD CHINESE GIRL, BUT I AM AN AMERICAN AND I CAN'T ACCEPT ALL OLD CHINESE WAYS.

—Flora Belle Jan, from The Chinese Americans *by Benson Tong, 2000*

Chinese American women worked as nurses in World War I.

ANGEL ISLAND

Beginning in 1910, Chinese immigrants to the West Coast had to stop at the Angel Island Immigration Station before landing in the mainland United States. The station was located on Angel Island in San Francisco Bay. Thousands of Chinese passed through the station between 1910 and 1940. Immigrants had to answer many questions, and sometimes they had to stay at the station for weeks or months. Some people were turned away because they did not have family in America, because they were seriously ill, or for other reasons. They were not allowed to enter the United States. They were sent back to China.

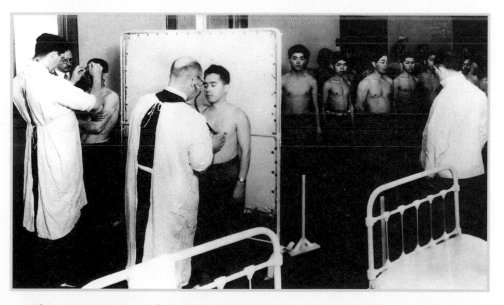

Chinese immigrants who came to San Francisco between 1910 and 1940 entered at the Angel Island Immigration Station. Doctors examined new arrivals to make sure they were healthy. Visit www.inamericabooks.com for links to more Angel Island information.

In the 1930s, the Great Depression brought further struggles. The Depression was a serious economic slowdown. Chinese Americans struggled along with the rest of the nation. Thousands of people lost their jobs. Businesses went bankrupt. Many families depended on donations of food and clothes to survive. But even with Chinatowns' uncertain future, residents did their best to help each other through the hard times.

WAR AND PEACE

In 1941 the United States entered World War II. China was also involved in the war, fighting on the same side as the United States. Many Chinese Americans joined in the U.S. war effort. They served in the armed forces, raised money for the war, and worked in factories on the home front. Most Chinese women in America had never worked outside the home before.

A Chinese American drafted to fight in World War II enjoys time with his family before he has to report for duty.

They got the chance to do so during the war, when businesses were short of workers. Many Chinese women came to like being in the workplace, where they met new people and learned new skills.

Chinese Americans' loyalty and hard work during the war gained them new respect from

their fellow Americans. The U.S. government decided to take another look at the country's immigration rules. A law in 1943 got rid of the old Chinese exclusion laws. Chinese people in the United States gained the same rights to become citizens as other immigrants. The bill also allowed a limited number of Chinese to immigrate into the United States each year.

World War II ended in 1945. Although it had been a terrible conflict, it had also brought Chinese Americans new rights.

CHANGES AND CHALLENGES

Dramatic events in China soon affected Chinese communities in America. A revolution took place in 1949, when Chinese politicians, led by a man named Mao Zedong, formed the People's Republic of China (PRC). The PRC was a Communist nation. Communism is a political system that is based on the idea of shared property. In a Communist country, the government owns all of the nation's land, money, and other resources. Individual people depend on the government to give them jobs, homes, and other things that they need.

Communist China also had new rules, and people's freedom was limited in many ways. Authors and artists were not allowed to express themselves openly. The Chinese Communist Party, which was the political group that controlled the government, had to approve everything that book publishers and newspapers printed. People could be punished harshly for speaking out against the new system or the new leaders.

Many Chinese hated the strict Communist government. They disagreed with its leaders and their ideas. Some of these people were able to leave China. They included students, teachers, writers, artists, and political figures. Many of them came to America.

But Communism was causing a stir in America too. At that time, the U.S. government and many U.S.

citizens distrusted the Communist system. Communism was very different from America's government and way of life. China and the Soviet Union (a nation made up of republics, including Russia) both had Communist governments. These countries were also two of the biggest in the world. Many people were afraid that if Communist nations became too powerful they might attack the United States.

These worries led to a period of suspicion and fear in the 1940s and 1950s. The government passed laws to crack down on Communist ideas in America. One law said that adult "alien residents" of the United States had to tell the government what their official political ideas were. "Alien residents" included Chinese immigrants who were not American citizens. Another law made it illegal to support groups that wanted to overthrow the government. Dozens of Americans

Immigration officers question Chinese immigrants suspected of being Communists.

faced trials for "un-American activities." Some of them went to jail. Many of them lost their jobs. People were afraid of having their friends and neighbors accuse them of being Communists.

Because of their heritage, Chinese Americans were often singled out as suspected Communists. They were accused of working for the Chinese government. They faced renewed discrimination and hostility from other Americans. Chinese businesses suffered, and U.S. authorities interviewed thousands of Chinese Americans about their political views and their loyalty.

Meanwhile, another conflict with Communism arose outside the United States. The Asian nation of North Korea invaded the neighboring country of South Korea in 1950, setting off the Korean War. Chinese troops joined the fight on the North Korean side. The United States joined the war to prevent South Korea from being taken over by the Chinese Communist forces. With U.S. troops fighting Chinese soldiers, Chinese in America once again had to cope with distrust and prejudice. A new law made it more difficult for Chinese to immigrate, and Chinese who were already in America once more had trouble becoming citizens. When the Korean War ended in 1953, Chinese Americans hoped that their long years of struggle would soon come to an end.

By the late 1950s and early 1960s, the situation of Chinese Americans had indeed improved. In 1965 U.S. immigration laws were revised once again. The new guidelines allowed more Chinese to enter the country and prompted the arrival of another wave of Chinese immigrants to the United States. Some of these newcomers were well educated and already spoke English. They often chose to settle outside of Chinatowns. Other immigrants after 1965 were family members of Chinese who had come to America earlier. These people were usually from rural areas and spoke only Chinese. The familiar feeling of American Chinatowns was reassuring to them, just as it had been to the first immigrants. The populations of Chinatowns across the country began to rise again.

In the twentieth century, Chinatowns all over the United States, including this one in Los Angeles, continued to help Chinese immigrants adjust.

The 1960s also brought a civil rights movement that swept across the United States. African Americans were fighting against the discrimination that they had faced for many years. Many Chinese Americans joined the movement to speak up for their own rights as Asian Americans. Parades and protests took place in Chinatowns around the United States. As a result of the civil rights movement, Chinese Americans became more involved in American politics and society. Their fight for greater freedom brought them closer to other Americans.

CHINESE IN HOLLYWOOD

Movies have influenced American impressions of the Chinese over the years. Moviemakers of the 1920s, for example, invented their own versions of Chinatowns and their residents. Most Chinese movie characters were either servants or villains. The evil movie criminal known as Fu Manchu was based on common U.S. stereotypes of the Chinese at the time. Some Americans thought that all Chinese were criminals.

The brilliant movie detective Charlie Chan was not evil like Fu Manchu. But Charlie too was based more on false ideas than on reality. He was shown as being timid but wise and mysterious. Chinese women were also shown in unrealistic ways. The movies usually made them seem beautiful but dangerous.

Many of these characters were not even played by Chinese actors. Charlie Chan and Fu Manchu were both played by white actors who wore makeup to make them look Chinese. These movies showed Americans a false image of Chinese immigrants in many ways.

However, as American attitudes toward Chinese Americans began to change, so did Hollywood images. More accurate portrayals of Chinese Americans have hit the screens in movies such as *The Joy Luck Club, Chan Is Missing, Pushing Hands, The Wedding Banquet,* and *My American Vacation.* Many of these newer, more positive films star actors of Chinese heritage and are directed or written by Chinese or Chinese Americans.

Meanwhile, freedom was becoming more and more limited in China. In 1966 Mao Zedong started a movement called the Great Cultural Revolution. The government encouraged people to punish anyone who did not support the Communist system and its leaders. Millions of people were arrested and imprisoned or sent to camps where they were forced to do hard physical labor. Many died.

After Mao died in 1976, a new leader named Deng Xiaoping took over. He made many changes to China's government. He decided that it was time to open up the country to more influence from other nations. He also wanted to loosen the Communist system's control over money, business, and trade.

But many Chinese were eager for bigger changes. They felt that some of the government's leaders were dishonest. Students and workers formed groups to fight for democracy. They held protests and spoke out against the harsh government policies. In 1989 a large demonstration lasted for days in a public gathering place called Tiananmen Square, in China's capital city of Beijing. But the peaceful protest ended in violence.

In 1989 protesters in Beijing erected a Statue of Liberty sculpture across Tiananmen Square from a portrait of Mao Zedong.

Government troops were sent to stop the demonstration, and the fighting that followed left hundreds of people dead.

TO FIND OUT MORE ABOUT HOW CHANGING CONDITIONS IN CHINA AFFECTED IMMIGRATION TO THE UNITED STATES, GO TO WWW.INAMERICABOOKS.COM FOR LINKS.

Meanwhile, many Chinese still struggled just to get by. Some of Deng Xiaoping's changes to the economy had made life harder for workers. In the cities, they faced low wages and unemployment. In the countryside, millions of peasants could barely raise enough food for their families. Most could not pay for health care. Few children were able to go to school.

Students, protesters, factory workers, and farmers all wanted a change. Many of them thought they might find what they wanted in America. They dreamed of greater opportunities and bigger incomes in the United States. But how would they get there?

WITH THE SNAKEHEADS

Back in the late 1800s and early 1900s, some Chinese immigrants had been so eager to enter America that they had paid smugglers to sneak them across the border. During the hard times of the late 1980s and early 1990s, smuggling became a problem once again. Limits on immigration to the United States still existed. Those limits meant that thousands of Chinese immigrants could not legally immigrate. Desperate to escape poverty and hardship, some Chinese turned to smugglers called "snakeheads" to help them get to America.

The snakeheads formed a network of people that smuggled Chinese into the United States. "Big" snakeheads were often Chinese who had already left the country. They organized the smuggling. They were also the bosses of the "little" snakeheads, who usually lived in China. Little snakeheads encouraged people to emigrate. They helped them find transportation and places to stay on their way to America. They gave them passports and other travel documents. Sometimes they even bought new clothes and shoes for immigrants so that they would look like well-to-do travelers.

But the snakeheads charged high prices for their help. Many immigrants paid thirty thousand dollars or more. This huge fee was far more than most Chinese could raise all at once. Most of them only paid a small part of the total amount before leaving China. The snakeheads told them that they could pay the rest when they got to America. It would not be hard, the smugglers promised, because work was easy to find and wages were high. They painted a bright picture of life in America.

Most snakeheads also promised that the voyage would be safe and easy. For a few of the smuggled immigrants, that was true. Some of them were able to fly straight from China to the United States. They were often nervous about what might be ahead of them, but their trips were not usually very long or dangerous.

But most Chinese faced a much harder journey. Some of them flew out of China but then had to stop in several other countries on their way to the United States. It could take more than a year to get to America, with stops in three or four or even more places along the way.

Others went by ship, just as the first Chinese travelers to the Land of the Gold Mountain had. The ocean voyage was still long, hard, and uncomfortable. Sometimes hundreds of people were crammed together in the lower decks of creaky old ships. If the ships had bathrooms at all for the immigrants, they were usually small and dirty. The air grew heavy and stale. The passengers had little to eat or drink during the long weeks of the journey.

Despite the **Golden Venture** *tragedy, many hopeful Chinese immigrants still arrive at U.S. ports on crowded ships.*

After crossing the ocean, some smuggling ships went directly to the United States. They usually arrived in the middle of the night to avoid being caught by U.S. officials. Small boats sailed out to meet the ships and carry passengers to shore. But sometimes they never made it that far. In 1993 a ship called the *Golden Venture* ran into a sandbar off the coast of New York. Hundreds of passengers jumped into the cold water and tried to swim to shore. Ten people died, and many more were badly hurt.

> *We sailed the ocean*
> *in the hold of the* **Golden**
> **Venture.** . . .
> *pigs chickens dogs snakes,*
> *whatever it was*
> *they called us.*
> *Our bodies not ours,*
> *sold to the "snakeheads"*
> *for the trip.* . . .
> *with the belief we could*
> *buy ourselves back*
> *for $30,000*
> *within three years.*
> *Our hard work would*
> *bring freedom*
> *to the next generation.*
> *Our sons would*
> *be prosperous*
> *and happy.* . . .
> *America needed our labor*
> *and skills*
> *as much as we needed*
> *its dream.* . . .
>
> —*Wang Ping, from the poem*
> *"Song of Calling Souls," 1998*

Other ships went to Canada, Mexico, South America, or the Caribbean. From there, immigrants still had to reach the U.S border and sneak across it. Many of them hid in large trucks that snakeheads drove into the United States. This journey, too, was uncomfortable and frightening.

Still other immigrants left China on foot, headed for neighboring countries such as Myanmar or Thailand. They climbed mountains and crossed rivers. They could only carry a few belongings with them, and they were often in danger of being arrested. The trip left them scared and tired, and they still had a long way to go to get to America.

After all the hardships that they had faced, many smuggled Chinese got as far as the border only to be turned back or arrested by U.S. immigration officials. But tens of thousands of smuggled Chinese immigrants did get across the border successfully, ready to start their new lives in America.

X-ray equipment at a U.S. border crossing shows that this truck is carrying illegal immigrants. Many Chinese immigrants first go to Mexico or Canada before trying to secretly cross a land border into the United States.

NEW STRUGGLES

Most smuggled Chinese immigrants settled in New York City's Chinatown. Their first worry was usually paying off the rest of their smuggling fees. Many snakeheads kidnapped people who could not pay right away. Because the new immigrants were in the United States illegally, they were not protected by the country's laws. They could not go to the police for help against the snakeheads. Instead, they paid the smugglers by borrowing money from family members and friends in the United States and back in China. These loans left them with huge debts.

Immigrants also soon found that not everything they had heard about their new home was true.

CHANGING CHINATOWNS

Modern Chinese communities are very different places from the old Chinatowns. Sometimes they are not even in the same place. New York's Chinatown swelled as Chinese immigrants continued to settle there throughout the last half of the 1900s and into the early 2000s. Eventually, many Chinese Americans moved to new Chinatowns in the New York boroughs (neighborhoods) of Queens and Brooklyn.

Other things have changed too. Bright streetlights have replaced dimly glowing Chinese lanterns. Movie houses have replaced classical Chinese theaters. Along with the abacus, the traditional Chinese counting device, stores also use cash registers. Shops sell American goods side by side with Chinese art. New Buddhist and Taoist temples share the neighborhoods with Christian churches and missionaries.

Distinctive Chinese-influenced architecture brightens Chicago's Chinatown.

Illegal Chinese immigrants often work in crowded garment factories such as this one in Manhattan's Chinatown.

Because most newcomers did not speak English, they had trouble finding good jobs. Often they could get only low-paying work in garment factories and restaurants. Many newcomers worked eighty or ninety hours each week and earned only three or four dollars per hour. Although this wage was more than most immigrants had earned in China, it could still take months or even years to pay off their debts.

With so little income, very few immigrants could afford good housing. Many of them ended up living in the same rundown buildings that early immigrants had rented. Sometimes ten people or more shared one tiny apartment. And even though they were surrounded by people, many immigrants were lonely. Most of them had left family and friends back in China. They made new friends in Chinatown. But after their long, tiring workdays, most people did not have much time or energy to socialize.

Yet even as Chinese immigrants discovered that living in America could be very hard, more and more of them took great risks to make the journey. As the new community grew in America, many people back in China began to feel even more pressure to emigrate—even if it meant going to the snakeheads. Sending a family member to the United States was a matter of pride. Families who had relatives in America had more money and were more respected than families who did not. Those immigrants who returned to China for visits seemed rich and successful. Young people worried that if they did not choose to leave, other villagers might think that they were lazy or not very smart. Because of these pressures, the snakeheads have stayed busy smuggling Chinese into the United States throughout the 1990s and into the 2000s.

OTHER STORIES

Although most newly arrived Chinese Americans have come to the country illegally, many of them have different tales to tell. Some have come as students or teachers. Some have valuable technical skills or medical or scientific knowledge. They come to work for American companies and hospitals. Others are

I'M AT WORK IN THE MORNING EVEN BEFORE MY EYES ARE OPEN. . . . IT'S MIDNIGHT BEFORE I RETURN HOME, BUT ALL THE MONEY I GET IS NOT ENOUGH FOR MY SUBWAY FARE.

—*anonymous smuggled immigrant, 1997*

writers or artists who left to find greater freedom to express themselves.

Another generation of Chinese Americans is made up of the children of immigrants who arrived in the 1980s or 1990s. Like young Chinese Americans in the early 1900s, they face the challenge of being both Chinese and American. They are proud of their heritage, but sometimes they feel embarrassed by their parents' Chinese ways. They want to fit in with their American friends, but they love and respect their families.

Many of these young Chinese Americans have never been to China. For a long time, it was difficult for their families to go back to their homeland. But in the early 2000s, the United States and China are building a more open relationship than they have had in the past. More U.S. companies are starting to do business in China. More Americans are traveling to China to visit.

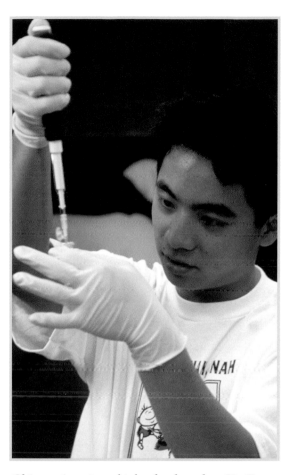

Chinese American high school student Yu-Fong Hong conducts a test for a study of cancer-related genes. He is one of the youngest scientists to work on the Human Genome Project, an important study of genetics.

FIND LINKS TO LEARN MORE ABOUT THE MANY WAYS THAT PEOPLE OF CHINESE HERITAGE CONTRIBUTE TO LIFE IN AMERICA AT WWW.INAMERICABOOKS.COM.

This new friendliness between the countries gives Chinese Americans great opportunities. Some of them are helping American businesspeople learn about Chinese culture and language. Others finally have the chance to learn about their own heritage and history firsthand by going to China and seeing the land of their ancestors. Understanding more about where their families come from helps them as they grow up in America, bringing together their two cultures to form a new community.

Looking Ahead

The experiences of Chinese immigrants in America have often been painful and hard. Over the years, Chinese Americans have struggled against hunger, poverty, violence, and prejudice. In the 2000s, many Chinese still come to America illegally. They face dangerous journeys and heavy debts. Once in America, they have many challenges yet to overcome.

Some people believe that the U.S. government must work hard to stop the snakeheads and human smuggling. They think that illegal immigration hurts both the immigrants and the United States. Others feel that it is more important to protect all immigrants, whether they come to America legally or not.

Whatever the future holds, Chinese Americans have already made great contributions to the United States. Whether they came in the 1800s looking for

I WOULD LIKE THE FUTURE GENERATION TO BE INTERESTED IN THEIR CULTURE, INTERESTED IN THEIR TRADITIONS, BECAUSE IF YOU LOOK IN THE MIRROR EVERY DAY, YOU CAN SEE THE COLOR OF YOUR SKIN AND THE COLOR OF YOUR HAIR AND YOU SHOULD BE VERY PROUD OF IT.

—*Anne Chinn Wing, from* Reflections of Seattle's Chinese Americans: The First 100 Years, *1994*

While keeping alive old traditions, such as serving tea for the Chinese New Year, Chinese Americans of all generations also hope to build strong futures.

gold or in the 2000s with modern snakeheads, they have worked hard to make a place for themselves in their new land.

Chinese American influence is visible in many areas of modern American life. In New York, San Francisco, and other cities with large Chinese American populations, the streets ring with music and happy voices during the Chinese New Year and other festivities. Chinese Americans work in every field, from medicine and teaching to music and art, and Chinese American authors, architects, athletes, and entertainers have found audiences and admiration in the United States. Chinese American organizations and newspapers support local communities. Many Americans of all backgrounds enjoy dining at Chinese restaurants, and Chinese American chefs have created new dishes such as chop suey that adapt classic Chinese recipes to American ingredients and tastes.

This blending—of Chinese and American, and of ancient traditions and modern ways—is very important to modern Chinese American life. Just as Chinese Americans are proud of their past, they also look ahead with hope, and their triumphs, troubles, and dreams are all part of America's story.

FAMOUS CHINESE AMERICANS

XU BING (b. 1955) Xu Bing grew up in Beijing, China, where he studied printmaking at the Chinese Central Academy of Fine Arts. He has made sketches and woodblock prints, and he is very interested in the written Chinese language. Xu Bing moved to the United States in 1990, and his Chinese heritage continues to influence his art.

MICHAEL CHANG (b. 1972)

Chang was born in New Jersey. He learned to play tennis when he was six years old. Chang went on to become an international tennis star. When he was seventeen years and three months old, he became the youngest male player ever to win the French Open.

AMY CHOW (b. 1978) Chow was born in San Jose, California. She started doing gymnastics when she was three years old. In 1996 Chow and the U.S. Olympic women's gymnastics team won the team gold

medal at the Summer Olympics in Atlanta, Georgia. Chow won a silver medal for her performance on the uneven bars. She also loves to read. Her favorite book is *The Joy Luck Club* by the Chinese American author Amy Tan.

STEVEN CHU (b. 1948) Chu was born in Saint Louis, Missouri. His Chinese parents had moved there to go to college. Chu was very good at math and science, and he studied

physics in college. He went on to become a professor at Stanford University in California, and in 1997 he won the Nobel Prize in Physics for his research on atoms.

CONNIE CHUNG (b. 1946)

Chung's parents came to the United States from China in 1945, and Chung was born in Washington, D.C. She studied journalism at the University of Maryland. In 1969 she got her first job with a television news program. Chung was the first Chinese American to anchor a major network television station's evening news. She has reported on many historic events and interviewed many famous people during her career.

HIRAM L. FONG (b. 1907) Fong

was born in Honolulu, Hawaii, where his parents worked on sugar plantations. Fong picked beans, shined shoes, sold newspapers, caught and sold fish, and worked at a golf course to earn money for college. He went on to earn his law degree, and he worked as a lawyer in Honolulu until 1938, when he was elected to Hawaii's legislature. In 1959 he was elected to the U.S.

Senate, becoming the first U.S. senator of Chinese ancestry. Fong served as a senator from Hawaii until 1977.

DAVID D. HO (b. 1952) Ho was

born in Taiwan to parents of Chinese heritage. His family moved to the United States when he was twelve years old. Ho studied science and

medicine in college and went on to become a medical researcher. He lives and works in New York. His study of HIV/AIDS has led to better treatment for AIDS patients and more knowledge about the disease. Ho was *Time* magazine's "Man of the Year" in 1996 and was awarded the Presidential Citizens Medal in 2001.

JAMES WONG HOWE

(1899—1976) Born in Guangzhou (Canton) in China, Howe and his family moved to Washington State in 1904. After a short career as the only Chinese professional

prizefighter in America, Howe became an assistant to a movie cameraman. He was fascinated by the work and soon bought his own camera. He went on to work for many movie studios. Howe won Academy Awards (also called Oscars) for his work on *The Rose Tattoo* (1955) and on *Hud* (1963).

HA JIN (b. 1956) Born in northern China, Jin came to the United States in 1985 to go to graduate school. He went on to publish poetry, short stories, and novels. In 1999 he won the National Book Award for his novel *Waiting*. He teaches English at Emory University in Atlanta, Georgia.

DONG KINGMAN (1911—2000) Kingman was born in Oakland, California, but grew up in Hong Kong. After studying painting there, he returned to the United States when he was eighteen years old. Kingman worked at a variety of odd jobs and used his spare time to study art and to paint. He became famous for his watercolor paintings, which combine Chinese and American styles. Kingman's art has been displayed in more than fifty

museums around the world and has won many awards and prizes.

MICHELLE KWAN (b. 1980)

Kwan was born in Torrance, California. Her parents had moved to the United States from Hong Kong. She won her first figure skating competition when she was seven years old. Kwan went on to win gold medals at five World Figure Skating Championships and eight U.S. Figure Skating Championships. She also won a silver medal in the 1998 Winter Olympics and a bronze in the 2002 Winter Olympics. Kwan always wears a Chinese charm for good luck. Her grandmother gave her the charm when Kwan was ten years old.

ANG LEE (b. 1954) Lee was born in Taipei, Taiwan. He moved to the United States to study at the University of Illinois. He went on to film school at New York University, and he has directed several popular movies, including *The Wedding Banquet* (1993) and *Sense and Sensibility*

(1995). His martial arts movie *Crouching Tiger, Hidden Dragon* (2000) won four Academy Awards, and he is also the director of *The Hulk* (2003).

BRUCE LEE (1940–1973) Lee was

born in San Francisco, California, but he grew up in Hong Kong. He returned to the United States when he was eighteen years old. A master of traditional Chinese martial arts, Lee developed his own style of self–defense. He also used his martial arts skills in kung fu movies such as *Enter the Dragon* (1973). Bruce Lee's son, Brandon Lee, also grew up to practice martial arts and to appear in films.

MAYA LIN (b. 1959) Lin was born

in Athens, Ohio, to Chinese parents. Lin studied sculpture, and when she was twenty–one years old, she won a national competition to design the Vietnam Veterans Memorial. The memorial is a polished black stone wall engraved with the names of Americans who were killed in the Vietnam War or who are still missing. It is one of the most often visited sights in Washington, D.C. Lin's work also includes a monument in Montgomery, Alabama, in honor of the civil rights movement of the 1950s and 1960s.

GARY LOCKE (b. 1950) Locke was born in Seattle, Washington, into a family of Chinese heritage. As a boy, he worked in his father's grocery store. After he finished high

school, he went to Yale University to study political science. In 1982 he was elected as a representative from the state of Washington. In 1996 he was elected as the state's governor, becoming America's first Chinese American governor. Locke was reelected as Washington's governor in 2002.

YO-YO MA (b. 1955) Ma was

born in Paris, France, to Chinese parents. His family later moved to the United States. Ma began learning to play the cello when he was four years old. At the age of five, he performed in his first recital. At nine years old, he played in New York City's famous Carnegie Hall. Ma has recorded more than forty albums, both alone and with other musicians. He is considered one of the world's best cellists. He also works with young musicians and encourages them to develop their talents.

I. M. PEI (b. 1917) Pei was born

in Guangzhou, China, in 1917. In 1935 he came to the United States. Pei studied architecture at the University of Pennsylvania, the Massachusetts Institute of Technology, and Harvard University. He eventually started his own architectural firm in New York City, and he has designed the John F. Kennedy Library in Cambridge, Massachusetts, an addition to the Louvre Museum in Paris, France, and many other projects in the United States, China, and around the world.

AMY TAN (b. 1952) Tan was born in Oakland, California, to parents who had immigrated from China in the 1940s. Tan studied English at San Jose State University in

California. After college she worked as a business writer, but later she decided to try writing fiction. Her popular first novel, *The Joy Luck Club*, tells the story of four Chinese women and their Chinese American daughters. Tan has also written short stories and children's books.

VIENNA TENG (b. 1979) Born to Taiwanese immigrants in California, Vienna Teng went to California's Stanford University and became a computer programmer. But after two years, she left her job to become a full-time musician, recording her first album in 2002 and making her first national television appearance on "The Late Show with David Letterman" in 2003. Music is nothing new for Teng, who began playing piano at the age of five and wrote her first song at age six. She has been praised for her clear voice and intelligent lyrics.

VERA WANG (b. 1949) Wang was

born in New York City. She worked as a fashion editor for *Vogue* magazine for more than fifteen years. After leaving *Vogue*, she began designing women's clothes. Wang opened her first store in New York City in 1990. She sells wedding dresses, evening gowns, and other clothes. Wang, who once dreamed of becoming a figure skater, has also designed skating costumes.

JERRY YANG (b. 1968) Yang was born in Taiwan to parents of Chinese heritage. He grew up in San Jose, California. Yang studied engineering at Stanford University in California. At Stanford, Yang and his friend David Filo created "Jerry's Guide to the World Wide Web." This hobby eventually became the website and search engine Yahoo!, which is used by millions of people around the world.

LAURENCE YEP (b. 1948) Yep was born in San Francisco, to a Chinese father and a Chinese American mother. Yep went to school in San Francisco's Chinatown, where he felt out of place because he did not know how to speak Chinese. He began writing stories in high school, and he has written more than thirty books for children and young adults. Many of Yep's books are about Chinese American culture, and he often uses ideas from Chinese myths and legends in his stories.

TIMELINE

CA. 1,350,000 B.C.	Early humans live in China.
CA. 1700s B.C.	The Shang dynasty takes control in China.
551–479 B.C.	Confucius lives and teaches.
206 B.C.–220 A.D.	The Han dynasty rules China.
221 A.D.	Emperor Qin Shi Huangdi takes power.
CA. A.D. 300s–400s	Many Chinese begin practicing Buddhism.
618	The Tang dynasty begins.
960	The Song dynasty takes power.
1040s	Movable type is invented in China.
1279	Kublai Khan conquers remaining Chinese territories, following Genghis Khan's invasion.
1500s	Large numbers of foreign merchants arrive in China.
1644	Manchu rulers establish the Qing dynasty.
1839–1842	Opium Wars take place in China.
1848	Gold is discovered in California.
1851–1864	The Taiping Rebellion takes place in China.
1869	The American transcontinental railroad is completed.
1882	The U.S. government passes the Chinese Exclusion Act.
1887	Severe flooding of China's Huang River leaves millions dead or homeless.
1906	The San Francisco earthquake occurs.

1911–1912	Rebels overthrow China's Manchu rulers and found the Republic of China.
1914–1918	World War I is fought.
1924	New laws limit immigration to the United States.
1941	The United States enters World War II.
1945	World War II ends.
1949	The People's Republic of China is formed.
1959	Hiram Fong becomes the first Chinese American senator.
1965	U.S. immigration laws are revised to allow more Asian immigrants into the United States.
1966	The Great Cultural Revolution begins in China.
1989	Chinese troops kill protesters in Tiananmen Square.
1993	The smuggling ship the *Golden Venture* runs aground near New York Harbor.
1996	Amy Chow wins a silver individual medal and a gold team medal in gymnastics at the Summer Olympics in Atlanta, Georgia.
1997	Steven Chu wins the Nobel Prize in Physics.
1999	David Wu becomes the first Chinese American member of the House of Representatives. Ha Jin wins the National Book Award.
2003	Maya Lin helps review ideas for a memorial in New York City to the victims of the September 11, 2001, terrorist attacks.
2004	Michelle Kwan wins her seventh U.S. Figure Skating Championship in a row, setting a record.

GLOSSARY

BUDDHISM: a religion founded in India around 500 B.C. by Siddhartha Gautama (Buddha). The religion spread to China, and many Chinese Americans are Buddhists.

COMMUNISM: a political and economic system. In a Communist country, the government controls business, farming, and trade.

CONFUCIANISM: a philosophy based on the teachings of Confucius. Confucius was born in China in 551 B.C. He taught that good morals and proper actions are important.

DYNASTY: a ruling family. In China, power was usually passed down within a family for generations.

FONG: a meeting place in American Chinatowns

IMMIGRATE: to come to live in a country other than one's homeland. A person who immigrates is called an immigrant.

MISSIONARY: a person who works for a church or religious group and tries to convert other people to his or her religion.

OPIUM: an addictive drug made from certain poppies. In China, opium was originally used as a medicine.

SNAKEHEAD: a person who smuggles illegal Chinese immigrants out of China and into the United States or another country

TAOISM: a philosophy followed by many Chinese Americans. The philosopher Lao-tzu began Taoism in China around the 500s B.C.

TONG: a Chinese secret society or association

TREATY: an agreement. Nations often sign treaties after wars to settle issues such as territory claims.

THINGS TO SEE AND DO

ANGEL ISLAND IMMIGRATION STATION
SAN FRANCISCO, CALIFORNIA
<http://www.aiisf.org>
The Angel Island Immigration
Station began enforcing U.S.
immigration laws in 1910. Newly
arriving Chinese immigrants were
questioned and sometimes held at
the station against their will. It
stopped operating in 1940, but
modern visitors can tour a museum
on Angel Island and learn more
about the station's history.

DRAGON BOAT FESTIVAL
BOSTON, MASSACHUSETTS
<http://www.bostondragonboat.org>
Boston has hosted its Dragon
Boat Festival—a traditional Chinese
festival—since 1979. Every June
hundreds of people watch the boat
races on the Charles River. The
festival also features arts and crafts
displays, dance performances, and
martial arts demonstrations.

MID-AUTUMN FESTIVAL
CHICAGO, ILLINOIS
<http://www.chicago-chinatown.com>
Chicago's Chinatown hosts the Mid-
Autumn Festival every September.
Sponsored by the Chicago Chinese
Cultural Center, the festival features
lion and dragon dances, martial arts,
music, and arts and crafts.

MUSEUM OF CHINESE IN THE AMERICAS
NEW YORK, NEW YORK
<http://www.moca-nyc.org>
This museum in New York's
Chinatown offers exhibits that
explore Chinese American life. The
museum also sponsors events such as
walking tours and mah-jongg nights.

NEW YEAR'S FESTIVAL
NEW YORK, NEW YORK
<http://www.chinatown-online.com/
nychinatown.htm>
America's biggest Chinatown holds a
huge New Year's celebration.
Attractions include food, music, and
parades. During the colorful lion
dance, the lion visits local businesses
to ensure a good year for the owners.

NIGHT IN CHINATOWN FESTIVAL
HONOLULU, HAWAII
<http://www.chinatownhi.com>
Honolulu's Chinatown kicks off its
New Year's celebration with the
Night in Chinatown Festival. The
festival features a parade, live
entertainment, and delicious food.

SOURCE NOTES

8   Confucius, *The Analects of Confucius*, n.d., <http://afpc.asso .fr/wengu/wg/wengu.php?l=Lu nyu&no=6:8> (April 5, 2004).

15   Lin Tse-Hsü, "Letter to Queen Victoria, 1839," Chinese Cultural Studies, n.d., <http://acc6.its .brooklyn.cuny.edu/~phalsall/ texts/com-lin.html> (April 5, 2004).

19   Ruthanne Lum McCunn, *Chinese American Portraits: Personal Histories 1828–1988* (San Francisco: Chronicle Books, 1988), 94.

22   Lisa See, *On Gold Mountain* (New York: St. Martin's Press, 1995), 3.

23   Jeff Gillenkirk and James Motlow, *Bitter Melon: Stories from the Last Rural Chinese Town in America* (Seattle: University of Washington Press, 1987), 44.

27   See, *On Gold Mountain*, 6–7.

32   McCunn, *Chinese American Portraits*, 116.

34   Gillenkirk and Motlow, *Bitter Melon*, 102.

35   See, *On Gold Mountain*, 9.

36   Ibid., 16.

44   Benson Tong, *The Chinese Americans* (Westport, CT: Greenwood Press, 2000), 66.

49   Tung Pok Chin and Winifred C. Chin, *Paper Son: One Man's Story* (Philadelphia: Temple University Press, 2000), 83–84.

56   Wang Ping, *Of Flesh and Spirit* (Minneapolis: Coffee House Press, 1998), 69–70.

60   Peter Kwong, *Forbidden Workers: Illegal Chinese Immigrants and American Labor* (New York: The New Press, 1997), 214.

62   Ron Chew, ed., *Reflections of Seattle's Chinese Americans: The First 100 Years* (Seattle: University of Washington Press, 1994), 10.

SELECTED BIBLIOGRAPHY

Chin, Ko-Lin. *Smuggled Chinese: Clandestine Immigration to the United States.* Philadelphia: Temple University Press, 1999. **By interviewing hundreds of smuggled Chinese immigrants, Chin explores their experiences.**

Haw, Stephen G. *A Traveller's History of China.* New York: Interlink Books, 1998. **This book surveys Chinese history, society, and culture.**

Kwong, Peter. *Forbidden Workers: Illegal Chinese Immigrants and American Labor.* New York: The New Press, 1997. **This book examines the lives of illegal Chinese immigrants in America.**

Los Angeles Chinatown. 2001. <http://www.chinatownla.com> (April 25, 2002). **This website for Los Angeles's Chinatown introduces visitors to the neighborhood's history, culture, and activities.**

Miscevic, Dusanka, and Peter Kwong. *Chinese Americans: The Immigrant Experience.* Southport, CT: Hugh Lauter Levin Associates, 2000. **This richly illustrated book explores Chinese immigration and Chinese American life.**

Pan, Lynn. *Sons of the Yellow Emperor: A History of the Chinese Diaspora.* Boston: Little Brown and Company, 1990. **This book discusses the lives and goals of Chinese immigrants to the United States and other countries.**

PBS. *Chinatown.* N.d. <http://www.pbs.org/kqcd/chinatown> (April 25, 2002). **This website about San Francisco's Chinatown offers photographs, history, and links.**

U.S. Census Bureau. "Profiles of General Demographic Characteristics." *Census 2000 Gateway.* May 2001. <http://www2.census.gov/census_2000/datasets/demographic_profile/0_National_Summary/2khus.pdf> (April 25, 2002). **This document provides details on American ethnicity and population.**

Worden, Robert L., Andrea Matles Savada, and Ronald E. Dolan, eds. *China: A Country Study.* Washington, D.C.: U.S. Government Printing Office, 1988. **This title gives a moderately detailed overview of China's history, society, government, and economy.**

FURTHER READING & WEBSITES

NONFICTION

Behnke, Alison. *China in Pictures.* Minneapolis: Lerner Publications Company, 2003. **This book introduces readers to the land, history, culture, and economy of China.**

Daley, William. *The Chinese Americans.* New York: Chelsea House, 1996. **Take a look at this book to learn about the history of Chinese immigration to the United States.**

Hill, Anne E. *Michelle Kwan.* Minneapolis: LernerSports, 2004. **This biography explores the life and sports career of Chinese American figure skater Michelle Kwan.**

Hoobler, Thomas, and Dorothy Hoobler. *The Chinese American Family Album.* New York: Oxford University Press, 1994. **Letters, diaries, and photos tell the story of Chinese immigration to the United States.**

Kite, Lorien. *The Chinese.* New York: Crabtree, 2000. **This book covers the history of Chinese immigration to the United States. It also explores the lives of Chinese Americans.**

Stepanchuk, Carol. *Red Eggs and Dragon Boats: Celebrating Chinese Festivals.* Berkeley, CA: Pacific View Press, 1994. **This colorful book introduces readers to a variety of Chinese holidays and festivals.**

Tagliaferro, Linda. *Bruce Lee.* Minneapolis: Lerner Publications Company, 2000. **This biography explores the life and career of film star and martial artist Bruce Lee.**

Yu, Ling. *Cooking the Chinese Way.* Minneapolis: Lerner Publications Company, 2002. **This cultural cookbook presents recipes for authentic Chinese dishes, including information about and recipes related to holidays and festivals.**

FICTION

Lee, Mill. *Nim and the War Effort.* New York: Frances Foster Books, 1997. **Growing up in San Francisco's Chinatown during World War II, Nim does what she can to help America in the war.**

Lord, Betty Bao. *In the Year of the Boar and Jackie Robinson.* New York: Harper & Row, 1984. **A young Chinese American girl in New York City adapts to life in her new country.**

Mak, Kam. *My Chinatown: One Year in Poems.* New York: HarperCollins, 2002. **Poems in a Chinese American boy's voice describe life in New York's Chinatown.**

Namioka, Lensey. *Yang the Youngest and His Terrible Ear.* Boston: Joy Street Books, 1992. **This book introduces the Yangs, a Chinese family who has immigrated to Seattle. Each of the four books about the family focuses on one of the children.**

Yep, Laurence. *Dragon's Gate: Golden Mountain Chronicles, 1867.* New York: HarperCollins, 1993. **In this Newbery Honor Book, a young Chinese boy, his father, and his uncle help build the transcontinental railroad.**

———. *The Journal of Wong Ming-Chung: A Chinese Miner.* New York: Scholastic, 2000. **Readers get to peek into the diary of a young Chinese boy working in California's gold mines in the 1850s.**

WEBSITES

CHINATOWN ONLINE
<http://www.chinatown-online.com>
This website provides information on the largest U.S. Chinatown, including details for visitors.

CHINESE HISTORICAL SOCIETY OF SOUTHERN CALIFORNIA
<http://www.chssc.org>
This website includes timelines, photos, and news about Chinese American history and culture.

INAMERICABOOKS.COM
<http://www.inamericabooks.com>
Visit inamericabooks.com, the on-line home of the In America series, to get linked to all sorts of useful information. You'll find historical and cultural websites related to individual groups, as well as general information on genealogy, creating your own family tree, and the history of immigration in America.

THE STORY OF CHINATOWN
<http://www.pbs.org/kqed/ chinatown/resourceguide/story.html>
This site from PBS presents a history of San Francisco's Chinatown, complete with photos, a timeline, and more.

INDEX

ACKNOWLEDGMENTS: THE PHOTOGRAPHS IN THIS BOOK ARE REPRODUCED WITH THE PERMISSION OF: Digital Vision Royalty Free, pp. 1, 3, 24; © Bohemian Nomad Picturemakers/CORBIS, p. 6; © courtesy of the Freer Gallery of Art, Smithsonian Institution, Washington, D.C., (accession #38.5), p. 7; California Academy of Sciences, p. 8; China National Public Import & Export Corporation, p. 9; © Brown Brothers, pp. 10, 14, 18, 27, 36; © KAREN/CORBIS SYGMA, p. 11; © Peabody Museum of Salem (#1518), p. 13; © Historical Picture Archive/CORBIS, p. 16; The Syndics of Cambridge University Library, p. 17; courtesy of Cornell University Library, Making of America Digital Collection, Putnam's Monthly, vol. 9, issue 52 (April 1857), p. 20; California Historical Society, San Francisco, p. 21 (#1002), 25 (#FN–22938), 29 (#12923), 33 (#25345); © Bettmann/CORBIS, pp. 23, 48; Library of Congress, p. 26 (LC–USZC2–3702); Adams Memorial Museum, Deadwood, SD, p. 28; courtesy of Picture Collection, California Section, neg. 912, California State Library, p. 30; Independent Picture Service, p. 38; © Minnesota Historical Society, pp. 44, 46; U.S. National Archives, p. 45; American Airlines, p. 50; © David Turnley/CORBIS, p. 52; © Reuters/CORBIS, p. 55; ©A&E/CORBIS SYGMA, p. 57; © Sandy Felsenthal/CORBIS, p. 58; © Mark Peterson/CORBIS, p. 59; © James A. Sugar/CORBIS, p. 61; © Phil Schermeister/CORBIS, p. 63; © F. Eisele/Action Press/Zuma Press, p. 64 (left); © Robert Tringali/Sports Chrome, p. 64 (upper right); courtesy of Steven Chu, p. 64 (lower right); Photofest, pp. 65 (upper left), 65 (lower right), 66, 68 (upper left), 69; U.S. Senate Republican Party Committee, p. 65 (lower left); © HASHIMOTO NOBORU/CORBIS SYGMA, p. 65 (upper right); Hollywood Book & Poster, p. 67 (upper left); © Frances M. Roberts, p. 67 (lower left and right); John F. Kennedy Library, p. 68 (lower left); © Nancy Kaszerman/Zuma Press, p. 68 (right).

Front Cover: Digital Vision Royalty Free (title); Library of Congress, LC–USZ62–56638 (center); © Bohemian Nomad Picturemakers/ CORBIS (bottom). Back Cover: Digital Vision Royalty Free.